50 WAYS TO ♥ YOUR PET

BY LISA TRUMBAUER
ILLUSTRATED BY DONNA REYNOLDS

For our nephews—
Wesley, Timmy, and Tommy Trutkoff and Jake Rowell
—L.T.

To my dogs—
Husker-doo Simon and the pit-bull girls, Sally and Lola.
—D.R.

This edition published in 2003

Copyright © 2003 by Troll Communications L.L.C.

All rights reserved. No part of this book may be reproduced or utilized in any form or by any means, electronic or mechanical, including photocopying, recording, or by any information storage and retrieval system, without written permission from the publisher.

ISBN 0-8167-7489-7

Printed in Canada.

10 9 8 7 6 5 4 3 2 1

Calling All Pet Lovers!

Do you have a Fluffy? Or a Rex? How about a Spot? (Personally, I have a Blue, a Cosmo, and a Cleo.)

No, these are not the names of the latest movie awards. They're the names of pets! And whatever name your pet has, all pets have one thing in common—they love their owners.

No matter what!

Bad-hair day? Your pet doesn't care.

Kicked the winning soccer goal—into the other team's net? No big deal to Fido.

Or maybe you flunked your math test. So what? You can do no wrong in your pet's eyes.

Your pet loves you unconditionally.

Now it's time to return the favor!

This book suggests fifty cool things you can do to show your pet how much you love him or her. Most of the activities are geared for that special dog or cat in your life. So if you have an exotic pet such as an iguana, taking Iggy to the leash-free park will probably not work for you. You know the special care your special creature needs. Don't feel you have to try every activity in this book if some are not right for your animal.

Which brings up another point—pet care. One of the best ways to love your pet is to take good care of him or her. Feeding your pet the proper food, providing plenty of fresh water, setting up appropriate housing, going to the vet for check-ups—these are all things you and your family already should be doing. So you're not going to find any of that stuff here.

Instead, you're going to find fifty nifty ways to do something extra for your pet. Have you heard of male or female bonding? Think of this as *pet* bonding! Choose the ideas you think your pet would really enjoy. Have fun with your pet, but always consider his or her safety and health, too.

I laugh when people tell me I spoil my pets. "Of course I do!" I exclaim. After all, why would I have pets if I didn't intend to give them the best life possible? I am fortunate to have three really cool animals—one dog, named Blue, and two cats, named Cosmo and Cleo. You'll meet my furry trio as you read the activities in this book.

Your pet is one-of-a-kind, and he or she thinks you're one-of-a-kind, too. Show your pet how special he or she is—whether you have a Rover or a Roscoe, a Lady or a Dolly, a Buddy or a Paddy . . . you get the idea!

What's in a Name?

Everything!

We're going to start off the book with something your pet should have already. But just in case he or she doesn't, we want to point out that it's the number-one way to show your pet how much you love him or her.

Ready? Here goes. . . .

Make sure your pet has a *name tag!*

Sounds simple enough. But you'd be surprised how many people don't have name tags on their pets' collars. A name tag is important. Even if your pet stays mostly inside or goes outside only on a leash, there is always the possibility that he or she could get loose—and lost.

How will your pet find his or her way home without a name tag?

So, if you don't have one already, before you do anything else, please get a name tag for your dog or cat. (Most pet stores have machines that will make a name tag for you.) Be sure to put your phone number on the tag. This way, if your pet runs off, someone can easily contact you when he or she is found.

Love your pet? Give him or her a name tag!

(Okay, we're done with the lecture.)

Make Your Bed

Getting a new pet can be exciting. You run to the pet store and buy all kinds of cool things, like toys and food dishes and chew toys, sometimes even a fancy, expensive bed.

But guess what? Your pet may be uninterested in the new bed. It may smell strange. It may even smell like other cats or dogs that were at the pet shop! So consider saving money by making your own cat or dog bed.

Here's a simple bed you can make for your small- or medium-sized pet.

1. Get an old pillowcase. Check with your parents to make sure you can use it.
2. Get some old shirts, towels, or other soft material you no longer use.
3. Place all the material inside the pillowcase.
4. Then sew up the pillowcase opening. (If sewing is not your thing, leave the open end of the pillowcase unstuffed and tie the ends together in a big knot, like a Santa sack.)

Now invite your pooch or feline friend to try out the new bed. Lay your head on the bed and call your pet over. Soon you'll be snuggling together, and your pet will know that this fluffy contraption is a special place just for him or her.

In Style

If you've taken your dog for a walk around town, you may have noticed the various collars worn by other dogs. Most of the time, dog collars are pretty standard looking. Collars or harnesses are made to be mostly functional, not to make a fashion statement.

Well, who says it has to be that way? Why not let your pet stand out with an eye-catching collar? No, you don't have to wander aimlessly through some upscale boutique, looking for the perfect style. Instead, make your own.

Here's what to do.

1. Get some fabric, string, lace, yarn—anything you can wrap around your pet's standard collar. (Be sure to choose a material that won't disintegrate if it rains. For example, taking pages from your favorite comic book isn't the best idea.)

2. Cut the fabric into strips.

3. Now wrap the strips (or lace or yarn) around the collar. Be sure to tie the ends together so the strips don't come off.

Voila! You've given your pet a collar or harness he or she can be proud of. This little bit of extra effort shows others how much you love your pet. And why not? He or she loves you right back!

Picture Perfect

Do you have photos of you and your friends doing cool stuff? Or maybe your family has pictures all over the house of you as a little kid. People take pictures for lots of reasons—to remember special times, to remember important events, and always to be able to see people they love.

So why not take pictures of the *animal* you love!

Ask a friend or someone in your family to take a picture of you with your pet. It doesn't have to be as fancy as the portraits taken of you at school. You don't need to go to a professional photographer and pose in front of a phony background. Go outside and sit on the front step. Put your arm around your pet and give him or her a big hug. Ask your friend to start clicking!

After the pictures are developed, choose your favorite and frame it. Put the picture in a place of honor so you and your pet can admire it. You could put it on your bedside table, hang it on the wall, even glue a magnet to the back and stick it to the refrigerator. Whichever you choose, displaying a picture of you with your pet is the perfect way to demonstrate how special your furry friend is to you.

Window World

Even though your home is a castle to your pet, he or she is still fascinated by what goes on outside the front door. Animals are careful observers. They enjoy watching other people and animals. Help your pet get that window seat to the world by setting up a viewing post.

If you have a cat, this can be pretty easy. Many cats can jump up onto windowsills, where they may sit all day. But not all windowsills are wide enough for your kitty. Instead, move the kitty's "tree" next to the window. (The tree is that shaggy carpeted thing your cat sits on or scratches his or her claws on.) This way, when Fluffy takes a catnap, he or she can still keep an eye on what's happening outside.

The same holds true for Fido. Since your dog probably doesn't have a cat tree, the easiest solution is to move a chair over to a window. If your dog is big enough, he or she can sit in the chair and get a grand view of the scene outside. Place a few pillows on the chair if the seat needs to be higher.

Yes, your pet loves to look at you—but he or she also likes to look outside. So go ahead and provide that window to the world.

Walk and Talk

Dogs love going for walks. As soon as you take out the leash, your dog probably gets excited, jumping and leaping like he or she has never done anything so thrilling before. (At least that's how Blue acts!) Going for a walk is a major event in your dog's day.

But sometimes, for us humans, the doggie walk feels like a chore. We have to take Paddy out so he can do his "business." Our day is already filled with tons of other stuff, like homework and school clubs and soccer practice. Therefore, we often ask our pets to hurry. After all, we don't have all day.

The next time you take your dog for a walk, try not merely to walk your dog, but to walk *with* your dog. Take the time to enjoy the walk, talking to your pet pal in the process. (Okay, if other people see you, they might think you've lost your marbles, but if it makes your dog happy, who cares?) For example, when your dog stops to sniff, say something like, "Hey, Em! What are you sniffing there?" Or as your dog trots happily at your side, talk about your day at school.

Not only are dogs great listeners (after all, they never talk back or give lame advice), but they can also pick up on emotional vibes. Need to get the walk over in a hurry? Your dog knows. Have the time to talk and walk? Your dog will know that, too. And he or she just might share a few things with you along the way.

Bandanna Bonanza

Have you ever seen a dog that wears a bandanna as a collar? Looks pretty cool, doesn't it? Dogs (and cats!) in bandannas are cute! Who knows why? Maybe it's because they look like little cowboys about to rustle up some cactus berries for dinner, then sit around the campfire and howl some tunes.

Here's a new twist on the old bandanna collar that your pet will appreciate.

You already know your dog or cat loves you. He or she tells you in so many ways—with licks, nips, purrs, and prances. One of the things your pet loves about you is the way you smell. A dog's or cat's sense of smell is finely tuned, much more sensitive than our own. And one of the things that gives us that special scent is the soap or shampoo we use.

So that your pet always has your scent nearby, soak the bandanna in a sink full of water mixed with the soap or shampoo you use. A half hour should do the trick. When dry, the bandanna will carry your distinct aroma. Wrap the bandanna around your pet's neck. Now your dog or cat can have your scent around, even when you're not!

Pick a Nickname

One of the first things your pet learns is his or her name. No matter how silly or dignified that name may be, your pet usually comes running as soon as he or she hears you call.

You say your pet's name in a variety of circumstances—when giving out treats, when teaching new tricks, when attending obedience-training school, even when you scold your dog or cat for doing something wrong. (Then you probably say the name in a gruff, serious voice.)

What your pet needs is a nickname! A nickname is a fun, special word you use when you and your pet are being affectionate. The nickname can sound like the real name, but it doesn't have to. We have several nicknames for our dog, Blue—Slappy (or Happy Slappy) and Puppy Shnuppy. (Don't ask me where these names came from—they just popped out one day when we were playing!)

And don't forget your cats. Our cat Cosmo knows when I say, "Cosmo Bosmo!" that we're overjoyed to see him. And Cleo is "Queen Cleo," of course.

Okay, we might sound a bit odd. But the animals seem to like it!

Phone Home

Is your dog or cat often left home alone? For example, maybe while you're in school all day, your parents and others in your family are at work. Animals can get lonely without their people around.

So why not reach out to your lonely pet by calling home and leaving a message? This works perfectly if your answering machine plays your voice as you leave the message. Simply phone home and call out your pet's

name. Say something like, "Hi, Blue! How's your day? We'll be home soon. Miss you!"

Of course, your pet can't answer the phone and talk back. (That only happens in TV commercials!) But he or she will be happy to hear your voice and know that you care.

Yes, it sounds goofy. But remember that your pet is used to the phone ringing and strange voices coming over the answering machine. The next time the phone rings, let the voice be yours!

Snack Time!

Many of us know that PB & J means *peanut butter and jelly*. So what does PB & P stand for? Peanut butter and pretzels!

This is a simple treat you can give your dog. No muss, no fuss.

Ready? Dip a pretzel in a jar of peanut butter. That's it!

So simple, and yet most dogs gobble it up! Dogs love to eat the things we do, but not everything people eat is healthy for dogs. So you have to be careful of the treats you give your pup. For example, chocolate, which most people love, can be harmful to your dog. So no chocolate ever!

But peanut butter is okay. Many dogs love peanut butter—and they make such silly faces when they try to lick the peanut from the roofs of their mouths.

Looking for that special doggie treat? Give your pooch PB & P—peanut butter and pretzels!

Catch a Nap

Does your pet have a special bed, or do you sometimes find your dog or cat sleeping on *your* bed? Many pets like to sleep where their owners do. In fact, you might even have found your kitty curled up on a shirt or other piece of clothing you recently took off and left there.

So what's the attraction? Why the bed or clothing?

It's all in the smell. Your clothing and bed covers smell like *you!* And being around your scent makes your pet feel loved and secure.

If your pet is not allowed to sleep on your bed, then make his or her bed extra special. Place an old T-shirt or towel on the bed. Your scent will linger on your clothing and entice your pet to lie there.

Sometimes our clothes smell a certain way because of the laundry detergent or dryer sheets we use. The next time you pull an old shirt or towel out of the dryer, place it immediately on your pet's bed. Not only will the material have a pleasing scent, but it will be nice and warm for your pet to snuggle into.

Happy dreams!

Take a Break

You're in the middle of a huge project. Or maybe you're studying for a major exam. Your brain is filled with all kinds of information—you feel like your head is going to explode.

Suddenly, your dog or kitty comes up to you, begging for attention. What do you do? Do you:

a. tell your pet to bother someone else?
b. give your pet a treat so he or she will leave you alone?
c. take a break and spend some time with your pet?

Sometimes the best answer to this dilemma is **c.** Our pets are perfect stress and anxiety relievers. And taking a few minutes to pet your cat, or even a few more minutes to walk your dog around the yard, has its advantages. It shows your pet that he or she is important enough that you'll stop what you are doing. It also provides you with a much-needed break, before your head really does explode—in the form of a headache.

Your pet can sometimes tell when you need a break. Show your pet you appreciate his or her timing by taking a few minutes for some extra bonding.

Body Language

Pets do really strange things sometimes. Like, what's with your cat rubbing up against your leg? Or how about that head-butting thing? Dogs also exhibit some weird body language. Like when they want to play, they scoot down in front and stick their rear ends up in the air.

There are many scientific theories for our pets' behaviors and body language. Whatever the reasons, our pets have a body language all their own. Much of a pet's body language is a way to show affection. It's the animal's way of saying that he or she likes you.

Express your feelings by speaking the same language—body language, that is!

For example, my cats, Cosmo and Cleo, love giving head butts. When I sit at my desk, they'll jump up onto my papers, then knock their heads forward into my chin. So I started doing the same—knocking my head gently into theirs. Not only do they enjoy it, they know I'm returning their affection as well.

Dogs can be a bit harder to imitate. After all, we don't have tails to wag. You can try this, though. The next time your dog gets into play position, do the same. Get down on all fours and prance around, just like your pup. Let your body language do the talking.

Knock Their Socks Off

Cats and dogs alike love stuffed toys. Our dog, Blue, chews his stuffed creatures until he's pulled all the stuffing out. Cosmo and Cleo tend to claw their stuffed toys and rub their faces against them. So what better way to express your affection for your pampered pets than to make a stuffed toy yourself?

Here's what you do:

1. Get an old sock.
2. Fill it with cotton.
3. Tie off the end with string.

It's as simple as that! Toss your sock toys to your pets. We bet it will "knock their socks off!"

From Plate to Bowl

When you have a cat or a dog, there is one mealtime tradition that is often hard to break—begging for food.

Because animals like to do what we do, they not only like to eat *when* we eat, but also like to eat *what* we eat. You might think it's cute when Aggie or Max sits and looks up at you with those big, "I'M STARVING! FEED ME!" eyes.

Of course, your dog isn't starving. And neither is your cat. (Yes, cats like to get in on the action, too!) Not only is it not good pet manners to beg for food, but also it is not healthy to feed your pet scraps from the dinner table. The main problem with this habit is weight gain. Because your dog or cat is eating more food than he or she should, your pet might gain weight, which can be unhealthy.

Even though we know begging is bad, we sometimes still like to share our food with our pooches and kitties. Perhaps you have a nice piece of chicken or steak, something your pet would really enjoy. What should you do?

Don't feed your pet at the table. Instead, every once in a while, wait until everyone has finished eating. Afterward, place a small amount of leftover food in your dog's or cat's food bowl. This way, your pet will know that he or she won't get food while you are eating, and you might just break him or her of the begging habit. At the same time, your pet will know that you do care and want to share your food. He or she will just have to wait until the time is right.

Running Free

Unless you have a fenced-in yard, your dog is often placed on a leash. It's probably a rare event if your dog is allowed *off* the leash to run around freely.

And there are good reasons for this. Keeping your dog on a leash keeps him or her safe. You don't have to worry about your pup running away or getting hit by a car. Walking your dog on a leash is part of being a responsible pet owner.

But doggies do like to run free. And the perfect place to let them do it is at a leash-free park.

Leash-free parks are starting to pop up all over the place. This kind of park is nothing fancy. Usually, it's just a large grassy area surrounded by a big fence. But dogs love it! Your pet will probably run around like crazy, sniffing everything and everywhere.

In addition, your dog will be able to interact with other dogs. Other dog owners bring their pooches to the park, and before you know it, it's a big pooch party. For the most part, all the dogs get along. If they don't, they have to leave. Those are the rules.

Check with your local park to see if it has a leash-free zone. (If not, why not suggest one?) You can also ask your

local pet store if it knows where the closest leash-free park is. You might need someone in your family to drive you, but your dog will appreciate it. (And *you'll* have a good time, too!)

Barkfest

Most dogs love to bark. They may bark when the phone rings. They may bark when someone comes to the door. They may bark when they hear a noise outside. Some dogs even bark at the TV!

What do owners usually say to all this barking?

"Shh! Quiet, Scruffy!"

That would be like someone telling us to stop talking!

Just as we enjoy a good gabfest, your puppy is sure to enjoy a big barkfest. For a few minutes, invite your dog

to bark at will. You might need to bark yourself to get started. Or maybe you'll have to clap your hands. Or perhaps ring the doorbell to set off your dog's barking. Once the barking begins, encourage your dog to keep going! Bark along! Let your dog bark until he or she is all barked out.

Dogs often bark when they are excited, so after your barkfest, you might have to calm your pup down a bit. Gently quiet your dog with a gentle petting and maybe a few treats.

But save some treats for your next barkfest!

Snack Time! Sandwich Roll-Ups

Here's a simple treat you can make for your dog—or even your cat!

1. Get a slice of bread.
2. Place a slice of sandwich meat on top. (My cats LOVE bologna!)
3. Starting at one end of the bread, roll it up.

That's it! No mess, no stress, and it's the perfect dog-bone size for a doggie treat. A sandwich roll-up may be too big for your kitty, so cut off some thin slices, and place the rest in a plastic food-storage bag. You can save it in the refrigerator to feed to Fluffy in the future.

It's always tricky giving your pet extra treats. Your vet will tell you to make sure your dog or cat doesn't become overweight. That's why a treat should be just that—a treat. Don't do it every day. A sandwich roll-up every once in a while should be something special for your pet to enjoy.

Can You Dig It?

Many dogs love to dig. Take them to the backyard, and they may start pawing furiously at the ground. Take them to the leash-free park, and they'll run around looking for the perfect digging spot.

However, usually we don't like our dogs to dig.

"It ruins the grass," your parents might say.

"It doesn't look nice," your neighbors might say.

"The dirt flies *everywhere*," you might say.

All of these are valid points. Still, your dog loves to dig.

Let your dog give in to his or her digging instincts by setting up a special area in the yard just for digging. This could be a sandbox you make for that purpose, or perhaps it's a section of the yard no one uses often. Instead of scolding your dog when he or she begins to dig, let your pup dig away.

Caution! Watch out for flying dirt!

The Tissue-Box Game

One of my cats plays a game that at first I found totally annoying.

Cosmo is what some people call a "shredder." He loves to shred paper. One of his favorite pastimes is sitting in front of a box of tissues and pulling out each tissue, one by one.

You can imagine my surprise the first time I came home and saw the floor littered with shredded paper! But Cosmo loves it, so now we make it a game. You can, too. Here's what to do:

1. Get a box of tissues. (Cosmo prefers the ones that come in a square box, with the tissues poking up through the plastic.)
2. Shove a kitty treat a few tissues down. (We usually show Cosmo that we're putting the treat inside so he knows the game is about to begin.)
3. Place the box in front of your kitty, and let 'er rip—literally!

Dogs can join in the fun, too. This works best with only a few tissues left in the box. Place a doggie treat inside the tissue box, and shake it around so your pooch hears it. Then place the box on the ground, and let your dog paw at the box to get to the treat.

Okay, so you might end up with a big mess. But the mess takes only a few minutes to clean up, and your pet will have a blast!

Level Love

How tall is your pet? A few inches? Maybe a foot or two?

Now, how tall are you?

It may not have occurred to you, but you tower over your pet. To your dog or cat, you're *huge!* Your pet always has to look up to see your face.

Every once in a while, get down to your pet's level. Sit on the floor instead of the couch. Lie on the rug next to your pet instead of having him or her lie at your feet. When you give your pet a treat, don't just stand there and bend over. Kneel down close to your dog's or cat's face.

Being bigger than your pet is one way you remain in control. Your size, as well as your tone and attitude, lets your dog or cat know who's boss.

But it's also nice to let your pet know that you're not so high up you can't come down to his or her level once in a while.

Just be careful—being on your dog's level means you might get that many more doggie kisses!

And the Winner Is...

Does your dog love to play tug-of-war? Ours does! He'll bring over one of his squeaky toys and toss one end into our laps. When we pick it up, he begins to tug and tug—and the contest is on!

The question, though, is who wins—us or him?

In most cases, you can probably take the toy from your dog with a giant pull. But here's a little suggestion, and if you take it, your dog will love you for it: Let your dog win!

Your dog loves to play with you. It's his or her way of connecting and bonding. At the same time, play can boost your dog's confidence.

And what better way to boost confidence than by allowing your dog to win? Not every time you play. After all, that would get boring. But every so often, let your pooch pull the toy from your grip, then congratulate him or her on being so strong. Your puppy-dog loves praise, especially when it comes from you.

Note: some experts don't recommend playing tug-of-war with a young dog being trained for obedience. If your dog is still learning who's the boss, play the popular game of catch instead.

Paw Prints

Here's a project you and your pet can do together—make paw prints!

Okay, so you don't have a paw. But you can make prints, too.

Get some art paper and water-based paint that washes off easily. (Check with a hobby or art store for suggestions.) Pour some paint into a shallow dish, such as a plastic margarine tub. As your pet watches, place your palm in the paint, let any excess drip off, then press your palm to the paper.

Now help your pet do the same. Gently pick up your pet's paw, dip it into the paint, then press the paw to the paper, right beside your handprint. Afterward, gently wipe off your pet's paw with a damp cloth or paper towel. Make sure the cloth is one your parents don't mind getting paint on. And make extra sure your pet's paw is *completely* clean before he or she wanders through your home!

Below your handprint and your pet's paw print, write your names and the date. Now, not only do you have a project you and your pet made together, but you also have a special memory of your pet. Hang the prints in a prominent place, or, if possible, place your paw-print art in a frame.

Snack Time! Cheese, Please!

Do you love cheese? Chances are your dog or cat (or even another type of animal) is a big cheese-head, too.

Here's the perfect way to please your pet's cheese craving: Sprinkle some shredded cheese over his or her food.

Whether it's Parmesan cheese you shake from a can, or shredded cheddar cheese you spread over tacos, your dog or cat will be in cheese bliss. You can even take slices of American or Swiss cheese, break them into bits, and add the bits to your pet's food.

The only thing you *shouldn't* do is give your pet a big chunk of cheese. If you've ever paid close attention when your pet eats, you may have noticed that he or she tends to scarf down food as quickly as possible. A chunk of cheese should not be gulped, because it might get caught in your pet's throat.

So liven up your pet's daily food every once in a while by adding a sprinkling of cheese. It's sure to please!

No More "No Zone"

Your pet loves being cozy. But sometimes the most comfortable spots in your home are also "no zones"—areas where the dog or cat is not allowed to be. No zones are often couches, chairs, perhaps even your bed.

Even though you may tell your pet "no," one day you'll probably find him or her sprawled across a forbidden no zone. Instead of getting angry, try a new strategy (with your parents' permission, of course). Cover up that no zone with an old blanket or towel. This allows your dog or cat the freedom to sit or sleep on that forbidden area, while at the same time protecting the furniture.

Like you, your pet enjoys being comfortable. He or she also likes to rest where you do, namely your couch, chairs, and bed. The best solution—and a perfect way to love and pamper your pet—is to cover up the favored furniture.

Home Alone

Chances are, your dog or cat is left alone at some point during the day. The time may be long or short. Either way, your pet might feel a little nervous or even lonely without any human companionship.

One way to ease your pet's nerves is to leave the radio on. It doesn't have to be loud. Choose a radio station that you often listen to, and choose a radio in a room where you and your pet spend a lot of time. Your pet will associate the radio and room with you. The noise will keep your dog or cat company, and, although he or she knows you're not home, your pet will feel comforted hearing something you listen to together.

In addition, leaving the radio on lets your pet know you will return. The sound of the radio becomes another link between the two of you. Your dog or cat might not think these thoughts exactly. For example, pets probably don't think, "Okay, the radio is on, so Davey is coming home soon." (Or do they?)

But your pet probably will be comforted by the familiar radio sounds. So let your pup or kitty enjoy some tunes, even when home alone.

Stormy Weather

Storms can be scary, even for people. A day that was once sunny suddenly becomes dark as storm clouds fill the sky. The wind picks up, knocking branches against windows and the sides of your home. Thunder rumbles in the distance, lightning starts to flash, and rain begins to fall.

Yikes! It's like a horror movie for some of us. For some pets, too.

Not many pets enjoy a fierce thunderstorm. The most important thing you can do for your dog or cat during a storm is to make sure he or she is inside your home.

The next thing you can do is comfort your pooch or kitty. Talk to your pet. Say pleasant things in a soothing tone. Assure your animal that he or she is safe.

Pets react to storms in different ways. I once had two cats, Alex and Rodney, who would hide under the bed during a storm. The two cats I have now, Cosmo and Cleo, jump into my lap when they hear thunder. Blue sits close by with his ears back, looking up at me, like, "What now?"

Tell your pet it's going to be okay. You'll all make it through the storm together.

28

Walk This Way

Your dog's walk is probably a daily routine. Perhaps it's a walk around the block or a simple walk down to the end of the street and back. Your dog (or even your cat, perhaps) loves the daily walk and looks forward to it as much as . . . well, as much as you look forward to getting out of school each day!

But what do dogs love besides their daily walk? (And besides you, of course!) They love walking somewhere different!

You get bored doing the same thing over and over again, don't you? Your dog might feel the same way. To show your pooch you know how he or she feels, mix it up a bit. Instead of going the same way around the block, walk in the other direction. Instead of walking one way down the street, walk the other way. Even walking on the other *side* of the street gives your dog something new to sniff and experience.

Just remember that where you walk is always a safety issue. Before you change your walking route, make sure it's safe for both you and your dog. And *always* tell your parents where you'll be walking.

Ice Is Nice

This special doggie or kitty treat is so simple, all you have to do is pour water. In fact, you might not even have to do that if you already have ice cubes in your freezer.

That's right, ice cubes! Ice cubes are not only a fun treat on a hot day, they're actually a terrific toy as well.

Here's what you do.

1. Get an ice cube from the freezer.
2. Put it on the floor (a floor without carpeting).
3. Push it around to make it move.

That's it! Dogs and cats love things that move. Not only will an ice cube skid across the floor when your pet pounces on it, but it's a treat he or she can actually eat. Our dog, Blue, loves chomping on ice cubes, especially on a hot day, so make it a game. We push an ice cube across the floor, then watch Blue go nuts! Even the kitties, Cleo and Cosmo, sometimes try to get in on the action.

Just remember to dry the floor thoroughly after the game is over!

36

Go Shopping

Do you like to shop with your friends? Or perhaps just hang out at the mall and talk with your buds?

Your dog would probably enjoy such an outing, too!

"What? That's not possible," you might say.

And you're right, in the conventional sense. You can't bring Mitzie to the mall. But you probably can bring her to the pet store!

Many pet stores these days allow people to shop with their animals. As you stroll up and down the aisles of rawhide bones, doggie treats, and squeaky toys, you can ask your dog's opinion and buy everything he or she really wants.

Okay, that might be stretching it a bit. But taking your dog to the pet store is a fun time for both of you. It's also great for socialization. If your dog doesn't see many animals and people at home, a pet-store visit is a great opportunity for him or her to meet and greet others.

The next time your family makes a run to the pet store, invite Gertie to come along for the ride. After all, you're shopping for her. She'll love it!

Brushing Up

This activity might actually fall under the heading of "routine pet care," which we said wasn't going to be in this book. However, it will make your pet feel so good, we couldn't ignore it.

Basically, it's brushing your dog's or cat's fur.

It's simple and something you might already do. But why not do it more often?

Brushing your pet's fur has several advantages. Number one, of course, is that it keeps the fur clean and manageable. This is especially true if you have a pet with long fur. Brushing the fur gets out the tangles and any dirt that might have gotten stuck.

The second advantage is that it is soothing to your pet. You know your dog or cat loves to be rubbed. Add to that motion the bristles of a brush, and your pet will swoon with pleasure. Well, maybe not swoon. But your kitty will start to purr. And your pup will probably raise its head and smile happily.

Hide-a-Treat

Have you ever gone on a scavenger hunt with your friends or family? It can be fun, especially when you find the hidden treasure at the end.

Your dog or cat might also enjoy a scavenger hunt—when you're not home! You already know your animal misses you when you're gone. The next time you leave, hide a few treats in special places where your pet might find them, such as the doggie bed or the kitty tree. The treats can be little nuggets of dry dog or cat food, or special dog or kitty treats you have on hand. Don't put the food all over the house. After all, you don't want your pet to have a total foodfest! (And your parents might not appreciate pet food everywhere.)

Scatter a few special treats in the places where you know your cat or dog hangs out. Your pet is sure to enjoy the treats—and will know that you think he or she is special.

Water Play for Dogs

This activity is perfect for those hot and humid summer days.

You've heard of a kiddie pool? Why not set up a doggie pool? Actually, it can be the same thing as a kiddie pool—one of those big plastic things you might have had when you were little. (Be sure to use the hard-sided kind. Your dog's claws will tear an inflatable pool.) Set it up in the yard, fill it with water, and let your dog go wild! Throw in some plastic toys, and he or she will soon be sloshing through the water to find them.

If a kiddie pool is not available, a garden hose also offers a good cool-down. Don't spray your dog too hard—you don't want to cause any pain. But a nice gentle spray will cool your pooch off and make him or her do all kinds of goofy things. (Our dog, Blue, likes to run and prance around when we have the hose on.)

And if you're all *really* having fun, you might even be able to sneak in a quick doggie bath, too!

P.S.: Not all dogs respond positively to water. If your dog appears scared by it, don't force the issue.

Water Play for Cats

Rolling around in the outdoor kiddie pool or being squirted with a hose is probably not your cat's idea of a fun time. In fact, many cats shy away from water. But some cats find water interesting to play *with*, especially if the water has little bobbing things floating on top.

Here's a fun game to play with your kitty. Fill a bathroom sink about three-quarters full with water. Place little plastic toys in the water—toys that will float. Then perch your kitty on the counter next to the sink. As your cat watches, nudge one of the plastic toys so it bobs in the water.

Yahoo! Fiesta time! If your cat is like mine, he or she will think these moving, bobbing gizmos are the coolest things. Maybe not quite as cool as fish. But your cat will still probably swat at them just the same.

Cats love a good chase or hunt. Chasing down objects in the water is one fun way to interact with your kitty.

Doggie Dancing

Often, a dog's life is a quiet one. When you're not home, the house is quiet. When you are home, you might be quietly reading, eating dinner, or doing homework. Your dog knows how to behave during these moments.

But your pooch is always ready to play and do something rowdy. So one afternoon, why not turn on the radio and invite him or her to dance with you?

All right, that may sound strange. But your dog will love it! He or she often imitates what you do. If you go outside and run, your dog runs. If you lie down to watch TV, your dog lies down beside you. Your dog likes doing the things you do. And your dog likes being active.

So turn up some tunes and dance! Yes, you might look goofy, but this is about loving your dog. (We didn't promise you'd always look dignified!) Call your dog to your room, pick up his or her front paws, and start to dance. Before you know it, your dog may be dancing on his or her own. Okay, maybe not on two feet, but he or she certainly might be prancing around, maybe even barking!

Doing a doggie dance is a great way to break up the day—and you couldn't ask for a more enthusiastic dance partner.

36

Fetch—with a Twist

Our dog, Blue, doesn't normally fetch. We take him outside, show him a ball or stick, and throw it, and he goes off to sniff a bush. He's just not interested. Nope. Sorry. See ya.

However, we've discovered that Blue loves to fetch—when he hears a noise! Pick up a squeaky toy, and he goes bonkers!

My cat Cosmo is the same way. Yes, Cosmo is not only a shredder (No. 20), he's a fetcher, too. He loves plastic bottle caps. I tap one on the edge of a table, and he comes scampering up, waiting for me to throw it so he can fetch it and bring it back. Sometimes he bats it around the wood floor for a while, making even more noise.

So what better way to combine the traditional game of fetch with something your pet responds to—noise. Make some noise to get your dog or cat fetching. Fetching might seem a bit boring to you, but your animal may love it. And fetching is also a great form of exercise. Add a bit of noise, and your pet will become a fetching fiend!

Starring... Buddy!

In the eyes of your dog, cat, or other animal friend, you and your family are stars. Even though you may have tons of stuff you're interested in, such as hobbies and sports, the most important thing in your pet's life is *you*.

Instead of just being the star in your dog's or cat's life, why not make your pet the star of something you do—like telling a story?

No matter what grade you're in, you will probably have to write a story or essay for English class. Why not choose to write about your pet? Tell a story from your pet's point of view. Think about how your pet feels when you go off to school. What do you imagine your pet does while you're away? What might he or she be thinking?

When you're done, read the story back to your dog or cat. Yes, we know it sounds corny, but your pet will love it! Of course, he or she won't know what your story is about. Your pooch or kitty will simply love that you're taking the time to talk to him or her and saying his or her name.

We can't guarantee you'll get an "A" in English class (although maybe you will!), but you'll definitely be the star in your dog's or cat's life.

Blanket Hide-and-Seek

Long ago, when cats and dogs were wild animals instead of domesticated pets, they had to rely on their hunting skills for survival. Wild relatives of dogs and cats—like wolves and lions—are still big-time hunters today.

Perhaps that's why many cats and dogs love to play hide-and-seek. The game imitates hunting activity. And one perfect way to play hide-and-seek is with an old blanket.

Invite your pet to be the hunter and seek you out. Our cats love to do this. We place our hands or feet beneath the blanket, then rustle them around. Our cats go nuts! They pounce on the blanket and try to "grab" at us. And because our hands are covered up with the blanket, we don't get kitty scratches. Our dog, Blue, on the other hand, tries to get under the blanket to see what all the fuss is about.

Another play option is to cover up your dog or cat. Move your finger along the outside of the blanket, and watch your kitty try to get at you. Blue likes to bite the blanket, so we make sure it's one we don't mind getting holes in. (Old towels work well, too.)

39

Massage Therapy

A massage feels good, doesn't it? To have someone rub your shoulders—ah!

Your pet might enjoy a nice massage, too. You probably stroke your dog or cat often and scratch behind his or her ears. You know your pet likes it, because he or she always comes back for more.

As a special treat, however, why not try giving your pet a real massage? Instead of just stroking the fur, gently rub your dog's or cat's back and legs in soothing circles. Your pet will realize that what you are doing is more than simply patting him or her on the head—you're sharing quality time, helping to sooth away any fears or worries (although, we hope your puppy-dog or kitty-cat doesn't have much to worry or be afraid about!).

Help your pet relax with a tender yet firm massage. What a great way to show him or her how much you care.

Snack Time! People Crackers

You've heard of animal crackers? Why not try some people crackers! It's a simple treat you can share with your dog. Here's what you do:

1. Get two slices of bread.
2. Using a cookie cutter in the shape of a person (such as a gingerbread man), place the cookie cutter in the center of the bread and cut out the shape. Remove the excess bread so only the person remains.
3. Place both bread people in the toaster and toast.
4. Remove the toast and spread on some peanut butter.

Voila! People crackers! One for you and one for you canine companion!

The Dog in the . . . Box?

Did you ever play with boxes when you were little, especially really BIG boxes? The box became your own little world, a place to hide and play in, maybe even sleep in.

Animals often like boxes, too. Cats love to explore the dark interiors. Dogs like to poke their noses in to see what's inside.

The next time you get a good-sized box, put it aside for your pet. Place it on the floor and invite him or her to explore. You might put a treat inside, coaxing your pet to look farther.

Our cats, Cosmo and Cleo, love leaping in, then waiting until we put the box flaps down, closing the box slightly. Their little paws stick up through the opening, trying to swat us. When we dangle a piece of string down into the hole, they have a blast.

Another thing to do with a box is to line it with an old shirt or towel. Place your pet in the box and watch your dog or cat sigh contently as he or she snuggles into napping mode.

Giving your pet a box to play with is a simple way to bring him or her pleasure. Be sure to get in on the action, too!

The Cat in the ... Bag?

In addition to boxes, paper grocery bags are great for playtime. First, you need to make sure the bag has no handles. Your pooch and kitty could get tangled in the handles and be hurt. (You don't want to use plastic bags either, because plastic doesn't breath—your pet could get trapped with no air.)

Lay your big paper bag on the floor on its side, with the opening on the ground. Our cats don't need any coaxing to romp inside—they shoot right in. But if your cat needs some encouragement, gently tap the sides of the bag, inviting him or her to explore. Kitties love it! The bag is like a long, dark tunnel full of feline adventures.

Your pup might also like the bag, especially if you make it a game. Place several bags on the floor, side by side. In one bag, put a treat. Let your dog explore the bags to discover the treat.

Finding new ways to play with your pet is one way to show how much you love him or her. Make sure the game is safe, then have fun!

Holiday Happenings

Holidays can be stressful for animals. (In fact, they're stressful for people, too, sometimes, aren't they?) You might have lots of friends or family over, strangers your pet has never met before. The daily routine may have changed. You may have moved furniture around to make room for holiday decorations. Animals find comfort in the familiar. When their home environment changes, they can become stressed.

Pay special attention to your pet during holiday times. Make sure he or she understands that, even though the location of the doggie bed or kitty tree may have changed, your love hasn't. To show your affection, make a special holiday toy for your pet and place it in the new location.

For example, during Thanksgiving, you could make a stuffed pumpkin out of a sock. During the winter holidays, mold a candy cane out of cookie dough. Include your pet in the holiday festivities, rather than banish him or her to another room. Your dog or cat needs to know that, even though some things have changed, you care as much as ever.

Cuddly Clothes

Have you ever noticed a dog or a cat wearing a little outfit? Usually you see this in the winter, when a pet might wear a coat or sweater.

Most of the time, dogs or cats don't need much protection against the cold because they have plenty of fur to keep them warm. Yet sometimes a little extra covering is in order, especially if it is freezing outside. To keep your pet warm during those first few frosty moments when you venture outdoors, place a T-shirt or sweatshirt in the dryer. Let the dryer run for about 5 minutes. This will warm up the clothing. Then place the clothing over your pet. Now, when you go outside, your pet will stay toasty warm. Yes, the clothing will cool off, but by the time it does, your dog or cat will have gotten used to the cold air, and his or her body will have warmed up from walking. Dressing your pet in warm clothes before a walk outside is PPP—perfect pampering procedure.

45

Warming Up

Brrr! You and your dog or cat have just come in from a walk, and it's *freezing* outside! You make yourself a nice cup of hot chocolate to warm up. But what can you do to warm up your pet?

How about a warm towel! Place a dry old towel in the dryer, and set the dryer on regular heat. Let the towel tumble around for about 5 minutes. When you take the towel out, it will be warm but not too hot.

Now bundle up your kitty or pup, or give your pet a nice warm rubdown with the towel. If your dog or cat is like mine, the activity just might turn into a game. My kitties love to roll around in the towel. As long as you don't mind a few pulled threads, let your pet have fun. Not only the towel will warm up your pet, so will the activity.

If you've ever put on a shirt or a pair of pants that have just come out of the dryer, you know how warm and cozy it can feel. Aaaahhh, that's nice! Your pet will think the same.

46

Toying Around

Chances are your animal loves your stuff. No matter how many toys you might buy for your dog or cat, eventually your pet will find something in your room that he or she just has to have. Maybe it's an old stuffed animal or a prized doll. Maybe it's your baseball glove or an action figure.

Because your pet loves your stuff so much, why not show how much you care by *giving* him or her one of your old things. Find a toy that you no longer feel connected to, and present it to your pet as a gift. Give your dog an old ball to chew on. Let your cat toss around an old stuffed animal every once in a while.

A toy means a lot to your pet because it comes from *you*. Getting a toy from you is one way your dog or cat knows you love him or her. Giving your animal a toy that was once yours makes the toy even more special.

Whatever the Weather

Your dog—and maybe even your cat—loves going for walks. But sometimes the weather doesn't cooperate. Maybe it's too cold outside. Or maybe it's started to rain or snow. Even hot weather can be a problem.

You probably know what type of weather your dog enjoys. For example, our dog, Blue, hates hot weather, but he loves the rain.

When do you think Blue and I take our longest walks? Yep—in the rain!

One way to really love your pet is to pay attention to what makes him or her happy on a walk. Is it splashing in puddles and getting wet? Is it enjoying the sun on a warm summer day? Is it rolling around in the snow? When the day brings a type of weather your pet particularly enjoys, make a special effort to take him or her for a walk. Okay, so you may get soggy or sweaty or snowy in the process. The walk doesn't have to be a long one. Let your pup sample the weather he or she really loves, and watch how happy a dog can be.

You might find that you don't mind walking in the rain or snow or sun so much either, especially when you see one of those adorable happy-dog smiles.

Tell Me a Story!

Okay, this one may sound totally goofy, but it works!

The next time you have some quiet time, the next time you sit down to read a book or you really want to bond with your dog or cat, try this: Read your pet a story.

Yes, it sounds strange. But your pet will love it, for two reasons:

1. You'll be spending quality time together.
2. Your pet will hear the sound of your voice in a soothing tone.

Your pet *loves* your voice. He or she responds to it, identifies with it. Reading a story to your animal is a perfect way to make him or her feel happy and secure. Simply curl up with a good book, invite your dog or cat to join you, then read away. Before your know it, your pet will begin to relax and will probably drop off to sleep.

No, your pet isn't bored—far from it! He or she is enjoying being with you and feels loved. Your special feline friend or canine companion is content.

If you like to read, share a story with your best pooch or kitty. Your pet might not know what you're saying, but he or she will love listening to you all the same.

Snack Time! Tuna Treats

Most of the treats in this book have been for dogs. How about our feline friends? Give this one a try!

1. Get a small dish.
2. Put a spoonful of tuna in the dish.
3. Add some shredded cheese.
4. Mix it all up.

Yum! What cat can resist? (Actually, Blue seems to like it, too. Sorry, Cosmo and Cleo!)

Lots and Lots of Hugs

And the final thing you can do to love your pet?
Give your pet *lots and lots of hugs!*

Sure, it's corny. But what better way to express how much you love your dog or cat—or anyone, for that matter—than by wrapping your arms around him or her, announcing that he or she is the best ever, and giving him or her a big squeeze?

Your pet is awesome. Perhaps what makes pets so special is that they love us no matter what we do. We are the apple of their eye. We are what makes their world go around. They love us so much that sometimes they can't control their tail wags or head butts or throaty purrs.

And we can show them we love them right back. Along with all the everyday things you need to do to keep your pet healthy and safe—feeding, grooming, vet checks—you can do something special every few days to show your dog or cat how you truly feel.

Enjoy your pet and share lots of hugs, every day!